ALIEN

Les quiero, mis amores, a las estrellas
más allá de la luna.

Mavi Rose

3G Publishing, Inc.
Loganville, Ga 30052
www.3gpublishinginc.com
Phone: 1-888-442-9637

©2019, Mavi Rose. All rights reserved.

No part of this book may be reproduced, stored in a retrieval system, or transmitted by any means without the written permission of the author.

First published by 3G Publishing, Inc. (May, 2019)

ISBN: 978-1-941247-63-1

Printed in the United States of America

Because of the dynamic nature of the Internet, any web addresses or links contained in this book may have changed since publication and may no longer be valid. The views expressed in this work are solely those of the author and do not necessarily reflect the views of the publisher, and the publisher hereby disclaims any responsibility for them.

Table of Contents

v   Introduction

11   Chapter 1: The Marriage

19   Chapter 2: The Divorce

35   Chapter 3: The Alienation

51   Chapter 4: The Court-Ordered Reconciliation

Introduction

Te amo a las estrellas, más allá de la luna!... Those are the words I texted to my children when they had no words to return to me. I love them to the stars, farther than the moon. And that is how far I would travel for them.

Every word and every drawing in this book was created right in the middle of the most arduous tribulation of my life. In fact, my pen was the only thing that bled out the pain just long enough to keep its pressure from ripping me apart. It was the only thing that kept me breathing for one more day, one more hour, or even one more minute.

I have been told that the words I choose paint horrific pictures. They are certainly not the choice of words one would use in a professional courtroom. Those words must surely be an unexcitable denotation of dates and actions only; completely devoid of any emotional implications. And on the outside and where it mattered for the sake of my children, I maintained my composure quite well given the circumstances.

But on the inside, my soul was writhing in pain and I was suffering immeasurably. Alone with my pen, I could translate every emotion with vivid color. I want you to take this journey with me and see what I saw and feel what I felt; the raw human experience of loss.

I was a mother and a wife once. People, from the outside, saw perfection: the perfect house, the perfect cars, the perfect romance... And I tried profusely to make that my reality. I smiled and ventured off on family trips and built with my hands a beautiful home... But in the dark, in the places where no one could see, I nearly drowned in my own tears. He broke the things I loved, held me firmly by the throat, reminded me how worthless a mother and a wife I was. I lost my children far before they ever disappeared. Several times during our marriage he would have them lock themselves in a room away from me, and ignore me as I called out to them. "I can take them from you if you ever leave me!" he promised.

Domestic abuse is not just a blackened eye or a bloody nose. It is being isolated from your loved ones by way of manipulation and control; It is being degraded and belittled in private as well as in front of your own children; It is being kept up late nights with yelling and threats of divorce, infidelity and suicide until you are too delirious to stand up for yourself and resolve to begging for forgiveness for whatever transgression you could have possibly made; It is being told what to think and what to wear and not being welcomed to share your own thoughts and opinions; It is watching your own child be strangled or threatened and being too afraid to speak out against the injustice.

I stayed and prayed and begged and tried with all my might. But eventually the burden weighed so heavy that my physical body became too weak to hold it up. He pushed me away one last time after 14 years of this toxic behavior, and I let him.

I walked away with much sorrow, but I knew whatever was to come had to be better and more peaceful than what I was leaving behind. And in contrast, in the hidden places where no one could see, there was a quiet and a calm that surpassed anything I ever knew. I became beautiful and strong. But in the public, he watched and attacked and made my every move more difficult than the last. And in the daylight, in front of people and in front of my kids, no matter how profane his actions they were all blinded by his twisted words. He fooled them all, leaving only my own family and a few devout friends at my defense.

For years he tried to strip everything from me, patiently waiting for every open opportunity to strike. I persistently made sure my kids visited him during his court appointed time, kept my mouth bridled as to my feelings and thoughts toward him and tried to make life as simple as possible for our kids. Regardless, he persistently harassed me to the point that I frequented the hospital for what I thought to be heart trouble, nerve damage and vision failure. Little did I know that my sickness was a result of severe anxiety and stress.

Then one day, after 5 years, he succeeded. He found the perfect opportunity to take from me that which mattered most: my kids. They were convinced that I kicked them out and abandoned them at a moment in which I was appropriately disciplining them for disrespectful behavior (no doubt a behavior coerced by their father). They became angry and were encouraged to believe that they had been rescued from me and my tyranny. And conveniently it all happened at an age when my kids had become self-efficient and no longer needed assistance cooking or driving or caring for themselves. My usefulness had run out and so had my right to motherhood. I did not see or hear from my kids for seven months other than a couple of impassive phone dialogues that were ordered by the court.

Through much patience and rationale on my part, the law eventually recognized the situation and stepped in to reconcile my children to me. Only, they were not my children anymore, and I was not their mother. I was simply an unfortunate circumstance they would need to endure. I took it slow and allowed them their space and gave them my full attention as needed. But they were strangers and my entire family, group of friends and myself were deemed foes to their father, therefore foes to them as well. No matter how hard we loved them, there was always some action or choice of words that would draw them away again. Just as it had been with their father, there was no right answer.

I eventually lost my daughter completely to her father as she became of age and the courts could no longer protect her from her own choice. After spending a year with me, her last year of high school, she decided to return to her father and cut off communication with me. Before she left, she told me she had been holding in her anger the entire time and wished to not return to my home again.

My son is communicating much better and even seems warm at times. But I am still not "Mom". Since he is underage, he is court ordered to remain with me and to only see his father for limited periods of time through supervised visitation. His father has not taken one opportunity to set up a visitation, however, I am sure he has seen him against the court order in secret. Since the time of the divorce he has been violating every legal agreement we have signed and I don't believe this one would be different.

The thing about trials is that they make us stronger. I have survived and thrived through more than I ever thought possible. I have an impenetrable sense of self-worth, I am successful in my endeavors and I am experiencing true and healthy love. I am most sad that my children had to experience what they have, but I know they will be stronger as well when they discover the truth and begin healing.

If anyone is experiencing such a tragedy as having to mourn their living children because their innocence has been manipulated, don't give up! I live on day by day. And I take with me a story I encountered while browsing the internet for information on the subject of parental alienation. I watched a video of a daughter who had been alienated from her mother and realized it only after her mother's passing. Her mother committed suicide just weeks before she discovered the truth. This story inspired me to hold on. Your turn-around could be just around the corner. Don't give up and learn to love yourself enough to find joy and peace outside of this pain.

CHAPTER 1

The Marriage:
Drowning in Love and Spinning in Confusion

These poems were written by a wife drowning in love and adoration for her husband. I trusted with my whole soul that we were meant to be together forever. There were times my love for him was overwhelming and I could barely catch my breath. Still, he would question my devotion and passion for him. I was constantly trying to prove my love and to no avail.

Looking back, I can see how my mind was twisted by his words. It seemed as though I was endlessly begging for forgiveness for not being good enough or as good as the next woman. I had tearstains on my pillows and at times desperately wanted a reprieve.

Little did I know, though my children did not see most of the abuse that was taking place in my marriage, they did absorb it from the atmosphere. Little by little they learned to see me as the lesser of their father and I. I, too, lived by this reality.

Experiencing the vicious "idealize, devalue and discard" cycle of my toxic relationship felt as though I was being murdered and revived over and over again.

I felt as though my abuser were judging me harshly on every detail of my responsibilities, of which I had many, as he stood idly by at a safe distance. No sacrifice or amount of effort could ever appease his insatiable appetite for perfection or gain his affection.

03/03/01

It is for you whom I would walk to the ends of the earth,
I would suffer the wrath of the woes of ten men,
Swim seas that never meet the skies,
And bathe in the blaze of the most merciless flames.
If not for love,
Then for what would I do these things?
My heart yearns for the joy of your pleasures,
My ears echo with the sound of your rejoicing,
My eyes hunger for the very sight of your smile.
I do the things I do because you are me, And I am you.
The nurturing of your desire is the nurturing of my soul.

01/01/05

Sweet love faithful and true,

Though gray skies paint a somber hue,

I know He carries me.

I see one set of steps in the sand;

I don't always seem to understand,

I know He carries me.

All my dreams have faded into the midnight sky,

When I reach back for them, they pass me right on by.

The cold winds are blowing so mercilessly;

It chills my soul so deep within me.

Icy rains are dancing as if to mock my pain,

Darkness surrounds me.

When will I see the light of day?

Sweet love faithful and true,

Though gray skies paint a somber hue,

I know He carries me.

I see one set of steps in the sand;

I don't always seem to understand,

I know He carries me.

I can't see what's before me; the road seems to disappear.

Though I walk through the valley I know I need not fear.

I know His arms will catch me if ever I should fall,

Though I may grow weary,

He hears me when I call.

There's a new day waiting on the other side of the storm.

My heart sings of rejoicing.

Who am I to mourn?

05/12/05

Look at the wounds of my past,

See how they bleed,

God, why do they bleed if they have been taken from me?

Have I truly been forgiven?

Do you see every lonely night,

Every unheard cry,

Every time I believed I was nothing,

When I lost the trust of a friend,

When I thought every time that this was the end?

He ignores my scars to create new wounds,

But the new cut the old,

And still he cuts on.

04/03/12

There's something about imperfection,

I see in my reflection,

I can't seem to shake the stain,

Sometimes I wish it'd rain,

And wash it away.

CHAPTER 2

The Divorce:
Losing Everything and Finding Strength

These poems were written by a woman who lost everything she thought she was. I was broken-hearted and at the same time experiencing peace and healing that I never had before. I had to completely rethink my identity and release my former hopes and dreams.

In the midst of my reformation, I learned that the abuse would not end with the divorce. I was fighting a battle much larger than I could have ever anticipated. Alienation was on a slow and steady incline alongside a smear campaign and a long list of court violations. There were times I felt as though I wanted to lay down and give up the fight, but every time I was able to find the strength to get back up again and the divine provision to make it through.

This was the most painful time in my life, but also it was the point at which I grew the most and discovered I was the strong and powerful woman I aspired to be.

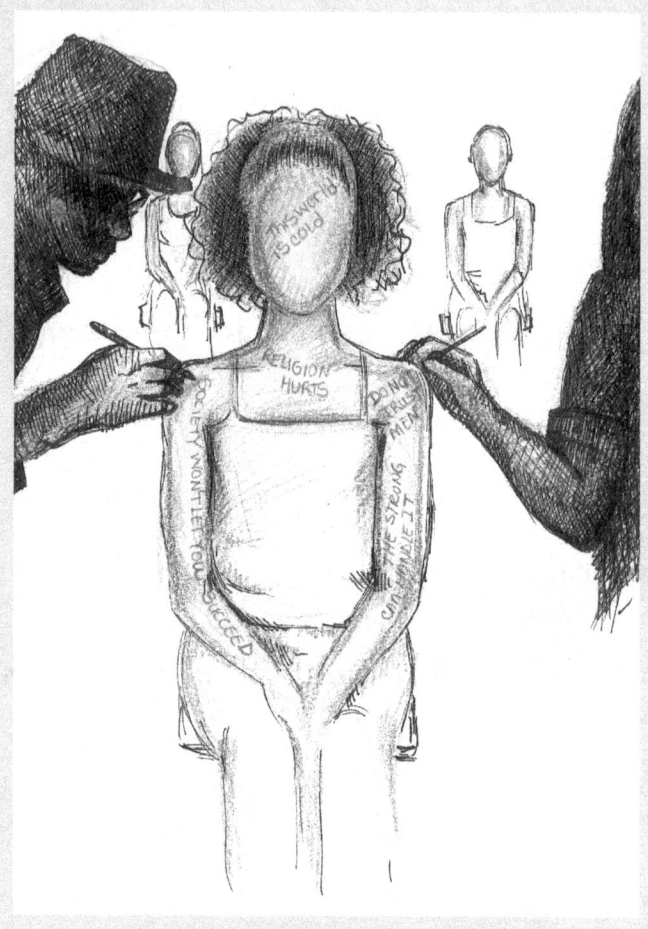

Children are innocent and free of bias, fear, and prejudice when they come into this world. It is we, adults, who write our thoughts and judgments across their hearts.

At the point of the separation and divorce, it became apparent to me that I would be stripped of my title and right to be "Mom". It also became clear that this process began slowly from the very start of our children's lives with shaming and insults against me that seemed minuscule, but shaped the very way they viewed me.

I began to get harassed in broad daylight instead of behind closed doors, like previously. I was harassed in front of police officers, school teachers and lawyers. No one either recognized it or attempted to stop it.

05/03/13

I thought today that I am slipping away,

I considered for a moment in time,

Handing over my own children.

I wish to be free;

Free of this perpetual torment.

I scream and no one hears,

I cry and no one sees my tears.

Every time my wound doth heal,

Again it breaks apart.

The most precious possessions of mine are my only bridge to torment.

05/03/13

Who am I now that I have been stripped of what I thought to be my purpose?
I am not a wife,
I may not be a mother,
I may not even be an artist.
Who am I now that I am alone?
There is only God and me.
What does He want?
I feel empty and have nothing to look forward to.
Could artists be so close to the creator in that they, too, create and it frustrates their reason?
The loneliness and purposelessness consume me.

06/19/13

The trees stand still.

Silence consumes me.

The earth is motionless.

Only the clouds wade along the sea of air.

I stand defeated and nature jeers at my surrender.

I am weak with wounds,

And soiled from the fight.

How oft I'd petitioned the God of Heaven.

How oft I'd fall and rise again.

How I endured the blows of this merciless beast.

Now I fall to my knees with flag in hand.

One more blow would have been my demise,

But from defeat I can still rise.

03/04/14

I once looked up and thought you tall,

Your stature towered above them all.

But then I realized I'd knelt,

Somehow,

In time,

My knees grew weak from shame I felt,

But now I know,

So I shall stand.

You are not taller than I am.

You shall rule me nevermore,

'Tis not my strength by which I soar.

03/29/14

I'd smile and wave at passers by,

While holding back the urge to cry,

Remembering just minutes before,

His icy words caused tears to pour.

I'd tell my friends I'm doing great,

Though I was kept up until late,

Afraid that night might be my last,

A slit, a gasp, or firearm blast.

Even after he had left,

His anger would not lay to rest,

I cried my tears still silently,

I honored him, though he not me.

I may lose friends and family, too,

But now I must reveal the truth,

Ladies out there,

Hold close my words,

It is not love if that love hurts.

05/27/14

Now I'm seething,

And you're just breathing,

But your breath brings death,

To the souls you're reaping.

My scars keep bleeding,

It's love they're needing,

But your hate can't wait,

To keep impeding,

Any hope I have,

For a soothing salve.

It's sad,

But my eyes stay fixed on the One who's leading.

07/07/16

Bittersweet,

Broken dreams,

Taste like honey,

And flow like streams.

The pieces fall,

Collect them all,

But never do they ever seem,

To place the same,

As how they came.

A masterpiece anew they shape, every time the pieces break.

07/25/16

Bend the bow,

And twist awry,

Strip its twigs,

And scatter nigh,

But beware,

For when it breaks,

Deaf ears will hear,

The sound it makes.

07/25/16

Can't see my bruises?!

Because they're too deep.

My soul has been tarnished by lies and deceit.

It's twisted and torn,

Battered,

Forlorn.

Though ice would be nice,

Only calluses form.

My heart is a tomb,

Each scar a tick mark,

Another is added each day in the dark.

Cold and abandoned,

Betrayed and misused,

Its old, rusted parts,

Have dismantled and fused.

No salve remedies,

Such a notion abstruse.

Still no bruise you can see,

But, alas, I am free.

Is it sadistic,

That I smile in the rain,

Broken to pieces,

Yet bastioned by bane?

Hurt though it may,

Turn blind eye if you wish,

I shall rise every time,

Though betrayed by a kiss.

10/28/16

Once upon a time,

I'd built a fortress,

Fortified with bricks of glass,

Each with letters of inscription,

That glistened,

At every pale moon's pass,

No eyes could read,

But those of he,

Who ruled my limpid fort,

He reigned as king,

O'er everything,

And me,

The gesture of the court.

I'd dance and sing a merry tune,

Regale until I'd fall,

He'd laugh with glee and say to me,

You haven't tried at all.

Go fetch a brick,

And build with it this fortress to the sky,

And on the brick of glass it read, I-M-S-O-R-R-Y.

I tried to climb as times ago,

But trembled at the task,

Insatiable was he who ruled,

This fortress built of glass.

I left that day to build anew,

A fortress made of stone,

No writing carved upon the walls,

But, "Unapologetically sole ruler of my throne."

CHAPTER 3

The Alienation:
Being Stripped of Motherhood

These poems were written by a mother who had to mourn her living children. I released them to their father in a time where he had so polluted their minds against me that they would be angry and want to leave regardless of what I said or did. I was worn down from the 18 year battle against abuse and manipulation. I was sure my kids just needed a moment to blow off their steam, and in the least I would be a part of their lives.

But for 7 months I neither saw them nor heard from them. Even when I received a visitation schedule from the courts, my children refused to see me and had to consult with or refer to their father's diction only.

I was robbed of my motherhood and all of my family and myself were reduced to watching the children's lives unfold through a computer screen. I was utterly broken, but even then, there was a spark of fight left in me.

When I was separated from my children, I felt as though my motherhood and every memory they had of me was being erased. I became to my children an incompetent,
unloving and irrational monster.

I felt like my children were being kept so far from me, and that their father's family and friends turned a blind eye. My kids were determined that they were acting on their own free will, but I knew all too well the manipulation they were under. I had been isolated from my family and friends repeadly during my marriage. I swore it was my decision regardingless of the fact that I had never separated myself from anyone prior to my relationship.

When I would run to the police for help they would tell me every time that they couldn't help me because they had to protect the rights of my children's father. The only way to get help would be to hire a lawyer and go to court. This saddened me because there are numerous women in this situation who do not have the resources and feel hopeless.

I would call and text my children during the time they were alienated from me, and they would not respond, except for a few isolated occasions when my daughter would answer the phone just long enough to find a quick offense and disappear again. I imagined that I was speaking to them while they were in a coma and waiting for them to come to.

01/20/17

I went through hell for you,

Crawling on broken glass just to,

Try to earn your love somehow,

And you don't even know my name.

Beauty is my name,

And you would never call it,

My love remained the same,

And yet you called me harlot,

But beauty is my name.

01/23/17

Deep wounds bleed true colors,

The conditional transition,

When they bleed black,

Cold as ice in the sunlight,

But when they bleed red,

They shine brighter in the sky's night,

Rising from the ashes:

Fire flight.

02/22/17

Be still your lips,

Compose them taut,

Let divulging words escape them not,

Conceal your tear-stained crimson eyes,

Cloak them under jovial guise.

To not a single soul reveal,

The bane that oscillates within,

For if they hear your torturous scream,

They will surely see the man I've been.

02/25/17

No seducer,

Nor spirit,

No narcotic,

Nor salve can remedy a broken heart;

One impetuously ravaged.

No escape avails,

How cruel a feat.

02/25/17

I'm dying,

And no one knows but me,

A bittersweet end to this epic tragedy.

I'm crying and though tears touch my cheeks,

I hold my head up high so that no one ever sees.

And I'm wounded but I keep my scars concealed,

If I wrap them tight and out of sight,

Only in time will my demise be revealed.

04/01/17

I cried out to the wind and in the end I heard a whisper,

I quieted my tears and listened close lest I should miss her,

"Sometimes they will return,

But only after you release,

Unseal your hands,

And hold your heart.

Embrace the rhythm of its beat.

That which is yours,

Will always be,

And in due time,

Those slumbering eyes will see."

04/21/17

Ink from my pen is running thin,

As I try to write away the bitter stains,

They're soaking in,

In an attempt to litter veins,

That otherwise bring oxygen,

To parts of me,

That keep me fully functioning.

This condition that I'm in,

It seems to keep on worsening.

I attempt to breathe,

But toxicity is drowning me,

Every time I'm inhaling,

"You'll never win",

I hear over my shoulder,

But I know they'll see the light,

In spite of how these days grow colder than they've ever been,

And yet I keep on pressing in,

You are the center part of me,

And for that fact I'll never cease,

Until you're in my arms again.

05/03/17

Erased,

Like a mistake in a letter;

Like a castle in the sand when the tide's high,

Like a falling star fading in the night's sky,

And I try to exist,

But you pass by.

And now I've dissipated from your mind's eye,

I died,

And I pray you resurrect me like the fire flight,

Of the phoenix whose subjugation is finite.

05/27/17

Wire and glue,

Hold me together,

Apart from you,

One glance,

One word,

One thing you do,

I come undone at the seams of me,

It seems to me,

The silence is a solemn key,

To keep the wire and glue,

From deep detachment at my extremities,

And in my organs, too,

They're functioning for now,

But that all depends on you.

Don't think that I'm too far to hear, I'm here.

I wait and watch to see,

The piece of you return to me,

That heals like salve and logically,

Can see my true identity.

06/01/17

I could not compete with the lie,

It shimmered like gold,

Brighter than all of the stars of the sky.

You were spellbound;

Captivated by the venom;

Serenaded.

So, frolic my love,

In the safety of,

One such beautiful lie.

CHAPTER 4

The Court-Ordered Reconciliation:
A New Beginning with A Stranger

These poems were written by a mother who had to reintroduce herself to her own children. It was a complete surprise to me the day the judge granted me permission to take my kids home with me from the courthouse. I was so appreciative that I would not miss my son's first day of high school or my daughter's senior prom.

We began a long process to healing that will take, still, more years to come. In the beginning they could neither look at me nor speak to me. At least we were able to come to a place where we could enjoy each other's company. However, I still long to hear the words "mom" or "I love you" or to feel a hug or a kiss on the cheek. They still do not understand the situation or know that I never had the intention to hurt them.

After a long court battle, their father put himself in a position to receive only supervised visitation by his consistent noncompliance and misconduct. While he is still potent in affecting the minds of those around him, and my children to some degree, I at least have the opportunity to make things right.

My lawyer asked me to go speak to my children during a court intermission, while their father was standing near. I had a history of experiencing severe panic attacks in his presence, and on top of that, I was anticipating another rejection from my own kids. I feel like few people can really understand the severity of such torment.

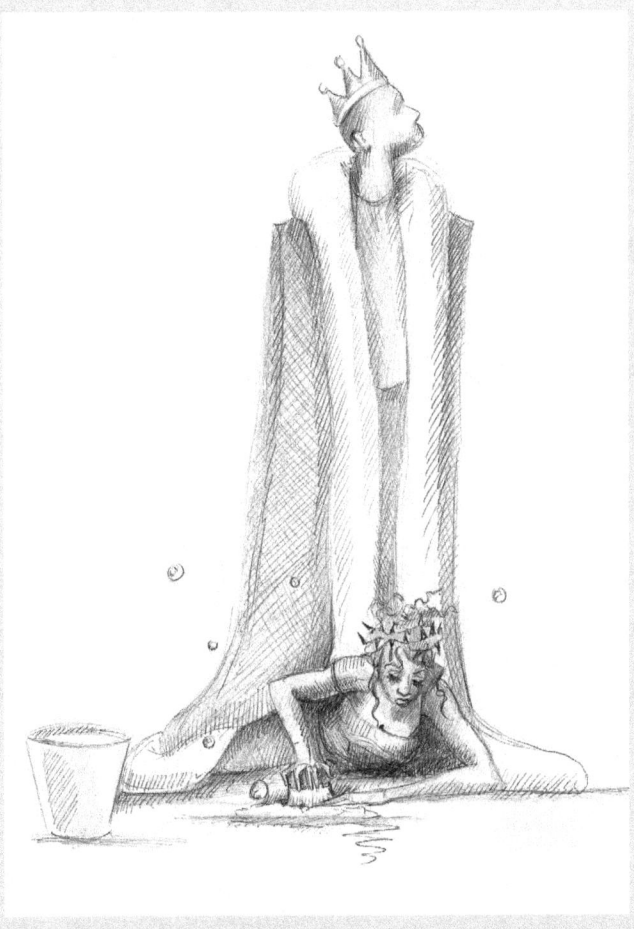

Since my children were born, I stayed home with them, toted them to their sports and activities, read to them at night before bed, took them on adventures and poured my heart and soul into them. Every memory and experience had been washed away. How I long to hear the word "mom".

06/02/17

From the inside out,

Just like you planned it,

You heartless bandit,

Your thievery is second to none,

And every time you steal another piece of me,

I swear that you've won.

But I'm not done,

Might not be able to run,

But I can crawl up to the finish,

In spite of missing a lung.

I'm breathing slow,

And bleeding fast,

By the bane of your blows.

I refuse to fall,

After it all,

I know you'll reap what you sow.

06/28/17

I am a broken vase,

Yet one cannot replace,

The vessel that I am,

For I was molded by the hand,

Of perfection and grace.

This crack is but a vein,

For new life to flow through,

Where that same hand goes to,

Remold and shine through.

The latter shape I take,

Will be greater than what I knew.

07/29/17

I'm pouring out my soul,

I'm bleeding fast,

And treading slow,

But it was I who left my cavity exposed,

I knew the cost,

And yet I spent it anyway,

I'd give my last on any day,

Because your worth to me is more than pay.

I will sustain in spite of pain,

I take my loss in hope for later gain,

For you I'll wait until the end of days,

Right now I am just wavering,

I'm feeling weak,

And yet I know I'm strong,

Only the boundless mother's love could bear to stand this long.

09/11/17

If I wore my wounds where you could see,

What then would you believe:

If I were adorned in blue and black,

With crimson streaming down my back,

What if I could barely walk,

Or part my swollen lips to talk,

If my broken bones pierced through my skin,

Would you believe my story then?

Sometimes I wish that this were true,

It matters not now what I do,

They've all turned deaf ear to my cries,

Ignore the tears welled in my eyes.

The scars of my soul you cannot see,

Yet they run deeper than the sea.

11/02/17

I can't breathe,

And I can't see,

And it's too tight,

And it's not me,

But they think so,

And if I let go,

I'll be someone that I don't know:

The face on the mask they strapped on me,

I want to take it off,

But have no key,

And if only,

I had one chance at freedom,

Then I would pour out my soul like the river to the sea.

01/03/18

Weary and broken by the bitter lies,

That spark rage in innocent eyes,

They are like venom,

Slowly draining life.

02/24/18

Love is,

Pushing back your tears,

Swallowing your pride,

Finishing your race,

After parts of you have died,

You've tried and tested every possible solution,

Released you right to retribution,

Been denied of absolution,

Absolutely drained of any strength that you could call your own,

You only survive just by the strength of grace and love that you've been shown,

And know that in the end if you have given all you have,

Come rain or shine,

Love is divine,

Do not regret your sacrifice.

04/06/18

He loves the blood I bleed,

The drops are bitter sweet,

He tastes them on his tongue,

He counts them every one.